Parade

by Terry Miller Shannon

illustrated by Chi Chung

Dean and Jada saw
the horses.
"I want to ride horses!"
Jada said.

"There's Mr. Grant!" Dean said.

"I want to make music,"
Jada said.

3

Next they saw dancers.
Jada did some steps.
"I want to dance," she said.

A band went by.
Jada said, "I want to play
music like that!"

Then they saw Mr. Lee.
"I want to be a lion dancer,"
Jada said.

"Wait!" Dean said. "You can't."

"Yes, I can," Jada told him. "I can do anything in the parade!"

Then they saw the balloon!
Jada laughed.
"But maybe not that!"